BOUND TOGETHERNESS THROUGH SERVICE

The Character Process Through Self-Reflection

JAMES O. FISHER-DAVIS

EQUILIBRIUM
SPORTS. EDUCATION. TOGETHERNESS

Copyright 2022

All Rights Reserved

No part of this work covered by the copyright herein may be reproduced, transmitted, stored or used in any form or by any means graphic, electronic, including but not limited to photocopying, recording, scanning or taping. The scanning, uploading or distribution of this book via the Internet without the permission of the publisher is prohibited, except as permitted under Section 107or 108 of the 1976 United States Copyright Act. To obtain permission to use material from this work, please submit a written request, write to: Equilibrium UP Rights and Permission Department, PO Box 2224 Matthews, NC 28106.

Bound by Togetherness Through Service
James O. Fisher-Davis

ISBN-13-979-8-9860751-0-5

Editorial Director: Twanna Warren
Assistant Editor: Carolyn Morse
Editorial Assistant: Jaymee Dawson
Marketing Program Adviser: Kywaun Warren
Design and layout: Jana Rade

For product information contact:
704-737-8704 or 704 288-8574

Equilibrium UP
PO Box 2224
Matthews, NC 28106
USA

Bound by Togetherness Through Service is a customized experiential product to be utilized within courses regardless of the discipline being taught. It may also be utilized during education and training sessions, retreats, seminars, for team building, relationship building, character and leadership development and more. Its overall purpose is to help everyone become the best human being they can be.

CONTENTS

Introduction 7

Chapter One: Choices Become Your Story 9
Chapter Two: Relationship Building 15
Chapter Three: Leadership And Opportunity 23
Chapter Four: Relationship Process 47
Chapter Five: Purpose 53
Chapter Six: Significance 59
Chapter Seven: Purposeful Experiences, Who Are You? . . . 65

Acknowledgement 71
Dedication 73
References 75

INTRODUCTION

Bound by Togetherness Through Service is designed to help individuals become the best they were designed to be. Everyone has a story, but when that story has a major impact on the life of an individual that story becomes their testimony. Once it becomes their testimony, the experience no longer belongs to the individual as it is intended to be shared to help others. Quite often, it can be helpful by providing **HOPE** to so many, **H**elping **O**ther **P**eople **E**xcel.

Muhammad Ali stated that, "Service is the rent we pay for existing on earth." There have been numerous iterations since 1978; however, it is a concept to which those called to serve should subscribe. It is virtually impossible to become a better human being and not serve others better, not treat others as you would like to be treated or not honor every human being in which you have interaction.

Carl Jung once said, "We are not that which has happened to us, we are what we choose to become." We make decisions everyday which impact us and the lives of others. Often these decisions are made based upon past experiences, information received, and quite frequently, our current situation and innate human desires. Our decisions become our story and we must decide what that story will entail and whether the fruition of our life story will be that which has happened along the way or the story that we choose.

How we serve others and how we see the idea of serving is often determined by the external, what an individual appears to be rather than who they are internally, their heart, soul, and spirit. Through self-reflection, we may be better prepared to see the *who* in our fellow human being as opposed to the *what*. Through shared stories, assessments and questions designed to provoke thought and self-reflection, the information in this book will offer the initial pathway and self-awareness assisting you in becoming the best you. Utilize the information to help build meaningful and sustainable relationships, unwavering character, and consistent leadership skills.

CHAPTER ONE
CHOICES BECOME YOUR STORY

It was 1963, there was a young 16 years old promising black male named Jack. His family and friends called him Jack of Diamonds. He was 6'6, handsome and the stories I've heard about him suggest that he was a great person, a great student., and a great basketball player. As is told, he scored 100 points in a basketball game. I think his coach and mentor at the time was Fred Taylor. One day after basketball practice as he arrived home, a friend of the family who was three to four years older asked Jack to ride to the store with him. Jack put down everything he was carrying on the front porch and jumped in the car to ride to the store. He had no reason to be concerned one way or the other because the family knew the young man. At some point in time, sheriff's deputies appeared behind the vehicle. Jack was unaware that the vehicle had been reported stolen. The driver fled with officers in pursuit. Near the Neuse River in Grifton, NC, an accident occurred at which time, as it was told to me, the deputies exited their cruiser pursuing the driver on foot. The impact threw Jack from the vehicle. Witness accounts were that Jack was near the river but appeared to be ok. To make a long story short, Jack died that day. Now from many accounts by people present, the family was told, and always believed, that Jack was drowned by two of the deputies who were on the scene. In 1963, you didn't really question anything; you just lived with the account that was provided to you, as a family and as friends. To this day, it still affects Jack's family. My grandmother had thirteen kids. My Uncle Jack was one of those kids. He was my mom's brother, but he was also her best friend. It was extremely difficult for her. Over the years, I heard the stories, but not all the particulars. There was always some ambiguity, which led to some ambivalence, as to exactly what transpired that evening to my 16-year-old uncle who had more than a promising future ahead of him.

As a young boy hearing this, surely there were a lot of different paths I could have taken and decisions I could have made. I could have had animus toward law enforcement. I could have not trusted law enforcement the way so many did not trust them and the way so many today are reluctant to trust law enforcement. That was not my tact. Because in the end, we all make decisions. We choose to go one way or the other. To this day, still not knowing the true account as to exactly what took place, I've come to understand my calling and my purpose in life which is to serve and protect and help as many individuals as I possibly can; to make certain individuals can trust those we give ultimate authority. I am referring to those tasked with serving and protecting every community and community members. I find my purpose in my family and so many of my family members, but I also find my purpose in my Uncle Jack and in my God. Not only did we lose him too early, but the world lost him too early as well.

SELF-REFLECTION EXPERIENTIAL:

1) Is there anyone in your life you need to forgive?

　

2) Why has it been difficult to forgive them?

3) Why are/were you reluctant to forgive others who have wronged you?

4) Who does forgiveness benefit most the one doing the forgiving or the one asking for forgiveness? Explain.

To reconcile takes two, however, only one is required to forgive. To forgive does not mean forgetting, it means that you will not hold a particular wrong against an individual. The ability to forgive while remembering the wrong that occurred demonstrates grace and mercy for another which also displays the highest character. When one has been wronged, they require something from the individual responsible for the wrongful act. When you forgive, you no longer require nor demand compensation or payment of debt. Forgiveness does not automatically lead to reconciliation, but we will not get to reconciliation without first forgiving. Forgiveness is our innate ability to grant mercy and remove one's actions as a catalyst regarding our future actions or reactions. In essence, if one wants to be empowered, then do so by removing baggage bestowed on you by others. The first step in life's road map is understanding that we must not take the journey alone. Most of us will ultimately be betrayed, hurt, used, and perhaps abused. Eventually, to be re-empowered and once again the captain of your ship and master of your soul, you must forgive. In order to move forward together it will require forgiveness, accountability, reconciliation and ultimately togetherness.

CHAPTER TWO
RELATIONSHIP BUILDING

I was four years old when my parents separated. A decision was made as to where I was going to go and who I was going to go live with. Perhaps one of the best decisions my parents have ever made was to leave me in Kinston, NC, with my grandparents. My mother was relocating to Philadelphia and my dad was relocating to New York. During that time, we always had contact and we always visited. The idea of living in the south, in the openness of the fields and in the fresh air, was appealing. Understanding certain things regarding nature and the process of growth as opposed to living in the city and experiencing city life was one of those things that gave me a different perspective and really helped form me and who I am.

I was predominantly raised by my grandparents, specifically my grandmothers. My grandfather James Fisher, for whom I was named, had a significant role in my life. He was a faithful and spiritual man who loved his family and sports. He took me everywhere with him to include the dirt racetrack and professional baseball games. He was a deacon at our church and sang with a gospel group called the Southern Spirituals. I ended up losing him when I was at the tender young age of nine. Along with my grandmothers, my aunts and uncles also helped raise me which meant there were always eyes upon me. One grandmother had thirteen kids; the other grandmother had seven kids. They were all extremely close and continue to be a close-knit family.

It was interesting because the house in which I grew up was situated virtually in the middle of the neighborhood. Ironically, I have often found myself in the middle or as a bridge connecting socially opposing entities. To the right side of the house was a field. In that field, if you know anything about farming, you know that farmers always raise different crops each season. Crop rotation included soybean one season, then planting corn the next season, then raising wheat and so on. I was always excited as I would sit there as a young boy and watch the farmers plow the land and fertilize and then go about preparing the soil for seeding. Then they would bring in other farm equipment that inserted and planted the seed in the ground. As time would pass, I was always able to sit there and watch the germination and watch the crops grow; you see it is a process.

On the left side of the house was a school. When I was younger, the school was segregated. One of the enjoyments I got out of life as a young kid was that I would go over to the school when school was out. I got the opportunity to watch coaches interact with a lot of student athletes. I watched track, baseball, football, and basketball practices and games. I observed how the coaches dealt with their players, how they went about the business of building them up and developing relationships with them, sustainable relationships. I watched them become mentors and role models to a lot of these student athletes. I admired them because in essence even though I was just standing there and watching, a lot of them later became my mentors as well. I attribute a lot of who I am today to those coaches.

During the summers, I would travel north spending time with my parents. I would spend half the summer in Philadelphia and the other half in New York. Individuals would ask me on occasion, though not that often, how I felt about the whole idea of living with my grandparents as opposed to being with my mom or with my dad. When I lost my grandfather, my namesake and someone whom I loved, adored, and admired, I made either a conscious or subconscious decision to live my life for him because I always wanted him to be extremely proud of me. I know he is always looking down at me and on me and that he has been an advocate for me up in heaven. When I lost him, there was some talk then about me going to live with my mom or with my dad. Even at the age of nine, I didn't want to make that move. I didn't want to make that transition. I didn't want to make that transition because, even at the age of nine, my grandmother had just lost my grandfather and I didn't want her to feel as though she was losing me as well. Even in my teen years, sometimes it would also come up, mainly because I was not necessarily doing the things I should have done. My dad would say that he thought it was time that I come live with him and my mom would say no this would be a good time for me to come live with her. At that time, I just felt that if I did go to Philadelphia or New York, that I would be choosing one of them over the other but most importantly that I would be choosing them over my grandmother and my aunts and uncles. They had been an imperative part of my life and had devoted so much in my development. For me, it was never really a difficult decision. There was never any animus that I felt, and I never felt sorry for not being with either my mom or my dad. I never blamed them with regards to anything or the situation. I don't know if I would be the individual I am today if I had decided to make that transition.

Nevertheless, one of many interesting things regarding my growing up in Kinston and in the fashion that I did was that I learned about relationships. I spent time during the summer in Philadelphia, in South Philadelphia to be exact. There was a lot of diversity to include Italians, Puerto Ricans, Irish and some African Americans. While there during the summers, I played with kids in the neighborhood and had an opportunity to see the kinds of relationships that my mom had fostered and that my stepfather had fostered. It may have been easier for my stepfather because my stepfather is Italian and, obviously, he fit right into the neighborhood. But I would notice on occasions when I was there, that there would be interesting looks cast our way. Mainly because my mom was an African American female, and my stepfather was an Italian male. They were often seen walking down the street or in the yard with a young black kid. My mother is one of the greatest relationship builders that I have ever known in my life. She has always gone about interacting with individuals based on who they are as opposed to what they are externally. Because I had a lot of relatives in North and West Philadelphia, surely, I spent a lot of time there. Those areas were more monolithic for the most part, consisting primarily of African Americans. My family is a huge family and a proud family as well. The opportunity to be in North Philly, South Philly and West Philly inspired me to consider the nexus that bound us all but at the exact same time, it was because of those experiences that over the years I've learned to navigate and cultivate relationships to the extent that I have.

Upon leaving Philadelphia, I would trek to New York. In New York, my father lived in Queens Village on Jamaica Avenue. We spent a lot of time in Queens and I spent a lot of time playing with kids there and watching my father and stepmother interact with neighbors and colleagues. My dad is a retired Sergeant Major and at the end of the day he had to learn how to navigate and cultivate relationships with various individuals regardless of their race or ethnicity or gender. My stepmother was a librarian/educator for the school system in New York City. An intellectual so to speak, an academic. She was also quite keen when it came to cultivating relationships with students, parents, and colleagues. Spending time in Queens as wells as in The Bronx and Brooklyn, and then leaving the north and returning to the south to Kinston, NC; all these experiences assisted me in what I do today, how I see the world and how I interact with individuals.

SELF-REFLECTION QUESTIONS:

1) What is the most important relationship in your life and why?

   _____
   _____
   _____
   _____
   _____
   _____
   _____
   _____
   _____
   _____
   _____

2) When did this relationship begin?

   _____
   _____
   _____
   _____
   _____
   _____
   _____
   _____
   _____
   _____
   _____

3) How did this relationship begin?

_____
_____
_____
_____
_____
_____
_____
_____
_____
_____
_____

4) What has been your most painful moment in any relationship? Explain what you learned from the experience and how it has impacted other relationships.

_____
_____
_____
_____
_____
_____
_____
_____
_____
_____
_____
_____

At the end of the day, life is about relationships. It is about relationships that you initiate and that you cultivate; meaningful relationships that you strive to sustain and maintain over the years. Relationship building comes with various tenets, certain things you must do for you to establish meaningful and sustainable relationships. Quite often they start at a young age. What is taking place, and what has taken place for decades, is that we have gone away from developing the skills, whether through the lack of teaching or organic experiences, causing the erosion of these skills over the years and we are experiencing the negative results today. We have gone away from these essential skills due to television, the number of channels that we access, social media and misinformation. We have gotten away due to computers and cell phones, to include texting. We have failed to invest time in one another to really get to know individuals by listening to them so we may learn something from them and understand their plight and gain a better understanding of who they are as opposed to what they are.

CHAPTER THREE
LEADERSHIP AND OPPORTUNITY

It was 1980. I was a high school student, 15 years old and growing up in Kinston, NC, which many deemed to be the basketball mecca of the world. Those individuals who were role models for me were my coaches and mentors. They felt their responsibility went well beyond just teaching us the sport or game that we were playing; they also went about trying to develop us into great young people. One of my basketball coaches, Coach Walton, afforded me and my team members with an opportunity that at the time seemed of little real importance other than being excused for a day in class; we took a road trip. We set out on this trip to meet two new head coaches in the Atlantic Coast Conference, which at that time was noted to be the best basketball conference in the nation. Those two coaches were Coach Jim Valvano, who was in his first season at N.C. State University, and Coach Mike Krzyzewski, who was in his first year at Duke University. Neither of whom had coached a single game in this ACC. This was not a camp, this was to be a one on one with our players, our team, and the coach.

Our first stop was Durham, NC, Duke University. We arrived that morning. I remember Coach K meeting us. We were not able to meet with the players initially, in part because Coach K had sent them off on a run. They would ultimately return from their run, meet back at the arena, and proceed with their morning practice for the day. During that meeting with Coach K, he talked about a couple of things. He talked about building a culture regarding his program. He talked about the pillars that would be needed and required to build that culture. He talked to us about character as a pillar. He talked to us about leadership as a pillar. He also talked to us about relationships as a pillar. He shared a lot of information with us that day regarding the pillars as well as how he would look to establish his culture at Duke University. We were extremely appreciative of the time he provided us. What I did not know at that time was the legend that he would later become. Nor did we know how successful the program would become. Over the years, I've had the opportunity to step back and watch them. To watch the relationship that he developed with his players. To watch the standards that he established regarding his players. I also watched individuals that he allowed to become a part of that program. I learned that it is not enough to ask the question. You must pose the right question. It's not enough to bring someone in, you must bring in the right individuals. And that was something that I learned from the conversation with him. When developing a culture, research would indicate that it normally takes four to five years for you to establish a culture or to change a culture. Duke had begun winning under Coach Foster but as with any culture it can always be improved upon. I think that we have evidence now that what Coach K shared with us were tenets that were true and, we can say now, accurate and assisted him in making Duke basketball what it is today. We did have an opportunity to watch the players go through their practice. They had a pretty good team that year. I do recall that one of the players, who was possibly the best player on that team did not return from the team run. The team was comprised of individuals from various backgrounds who probably saw life differently. Coach

K was able to mold those guys and build some cohesiveness. As I think back, I think that maybe that was the change of culture that Coach K was talking about. The idea of getting everyone to buy into what was expected. My guess, and it is only my guess, was that after that day, probably after that particular year, that whenever he sent guys out to run, that they all returned.

When we left Durham, heading back toward Kinston, we stopped off in Raleigh for a N.C. State men's basketball practice. Prior to practice, we had an opportunity to meet with Coach Jim Valvano for about 45 minutes to 60 minutes. Again, it was just our team, our coach, and Coach Valvano. It was interesting because there was information that he provided that I also was able to implement over the years. Coach Valvano talked about purpose and an individual's calling. He also talked about being passionate in what you do. He said, "Whatever you do, be extremely passionate about it. Wherever you are, be extremely passionate about it." Sometimes things would be difficult and, it's ironic now knowing what Coach Valvano went through and the battles he had to try and conquer the best he could, he talked about perseverance. I remember when he gave his speech and said the words, "Don't give up, don't ever give up." In essence, that was the exact same thing that he was sharing with us that day in 1980. Again, we had no idea who we were in front of; no idea what the coaches would do or what they would accomplish. Coach Valvano talked about hope. He talked about believing in something. He talked about believing in one another, faith, hope and love. This opportunity we were afforded occurred in 1980. In 1983, N.C State University men's basketball team won the national championship. This was an underdog team. This was a team that had talent, but they were an underdog team. There is no doubt in my mind that the reason they were able to win was because of the emphasis Coach

Valvano placed on perseverance. The emphasis he placed upon the idea of not giving up. The emphasis he placed on having hope in one another, believing and being extremely passionate regarding what you do and how you do it.

For me, even unbeknownst to me, these are all tenets that I was able to implement in my life after having an opportunity and now being so honored to be in front of two great coaches. Even though at that time they were not considered to be great coaches, they were just new coaches coaching in the best basketball conference in the country. But what I also recall, is that no they weren't Dean Smith or Coach Holland from Virginia who were established. They were coaches who were afforded an opportunity and they took advantage of that opportunity that they were given. I'd like to think that I also took advantage of an opportunity. I decided that their message was going to be important and I listened intently. I decided they didn't have to be Dean Smith or Terry Holland. I thought that it was just enough that they would take the time out to speak to 14, 15 and 16-year-olds. Not in a camp setting but just as an individual team. Another thing that I also took from this opportunity was that often we decide that we are not necessarily going to listen or pay attention to a message. Or that we are going to disregard the message because of the messenger. That is a mistake we make way too often. We can always learn. The interesting thing is that you never know who you can learn from. Those conversations were a part of what I believe to this day. They are a part of my fabric and my foundation in building relationships with others, and regarding character building and leadership. They became extended building blocks. Building blocks stacked upon building blocks from information that I gleaned over the years from other individuals who had an expertise in navigating relationships with others.

Answer the following questions below designed to assist you regarding who you are and how others may see you. Remember this is only a snapshot however, the goal is to point you in the right direction and place you upon the path toward improvement. Vince Lombardi said, "Perfection is not attainable but if we chase perfection, we can catch excellence along the way".

SELF-REFLECTION AUDIT

SECTION #1

1) Do you blame yourself for negative events that have happened in your past?
   ☐ YES   ☐ NO

2) Do you feel ashamed of the events that have occurred in your life?
   ☐ YES   ☐ NO

3) Do you often wish you could go back in your past and rewind time to fix the areas you went wrong?
   ☐ YES   ☐ NO

4) Do you ever wish you were never born because of the way your life has turned out?
   ☐ YES   ☐ NO

If you answered "yes" to one or more of the questions in this section, you may be dealing with issues of shame and guilt.

SECTION #2

1) When you look in the mirror, do you like what you see?
   ☐ YES   ☐ NO

2)   Do you feel confident about yourself and the direction in which you are going in life?
    ☐ YES   ☐ NO

3)   Do you constantly compare yourself with others around you and measure your standards against theirs?
    ☐ YES   ☐ NO

4)   Do you wish you could be someone else?
    ☐ YES   ☐ NO

If you answered "yes" to one or more of these questions in this section, you may be dealing with issues of self-pity and low self-esteem.

SECTION #3

1)   Do you blame a particular person or group of people for how your life turned out?
    ☐ YES   ☐ NO

2)   Do you often replay in your mind the pain that another has inflicted upon you?
    ☐ YES   ☐ NO

3)   Are you angry with someone who has hurt you in the past?
    ☐ YES   ☐ NO

4) Do you have rage and anger that appears quickly when someone does something to you?
☐ YES ☐ NO

If you answered "yes" to one or more of the questions in this section, you may be dealing with issues of anger, resentment and unforgiveness.

SECTION #4

1) Do you feel sad or lonely?
☐ YES ☐ NO

2) Do you cry when you think about your life and all that has happened to you?
☐ YES ☐ NO

3) Is it hard for you to be motivated to move forward in life because you feel heavily burdened by the weight of your problems?
☐ YES ☐ NO

4) Are you confused about what your next phase of life will be?
☐ YES ☐ NO

If you answered "yes" to one or more of the questions in this section, you may be dealing with issues of depression and frustration.

SECTION #5

1) Do you highly value what others say or think about you?
   ☐ YES   ☐ NO

2) Do you often seek the advice of another person before you make a decision?
   ☐ YES   ☐ NO

3) Do you often try your best to keep those whom you love or others around you happy?
   ☐ YES   ☐ NO

4) Are you uncomfortable when you are not in a relationship with a significant other?
   ☐ YES   ☐ NO

If you answered "yes" to one or more questions in this section, you may be dealing with issues of codependency and insecurity.

SECTION #6

1) Are you afraid of what the future holds for you?
   ☐ YES   ☐ NO

2) Are you frightened to take on new challenges?
   ☐ YES   ☐ NO

3) Do you worry about what may or may not happen in the future?
   ☐ YES   ☐ NO

4) Are you afraid of what others may think if you fail at a challenging task?
   ☐ YES   ☐ NO

If you answered "yes" to one or more questions in this section, you may be dealing with issues of anxiety, fear, worry and doubt.

SECTION #7

1) Are you sad when you see others attain achievements that you have not?
   ☐ YES   ☐ NO

2) Do you want things that you see others have?
   ☐ YES   ☐ NO

3) Do you dislike complimenting others on their victories?
   ☐ YES   ☐ NO

4) Are you judgmental or critical of others?
   ☐ YES   ☐ NO

   If you answered "yes" to one or more of the questions in this section, you may be dealing with issues of jealousy.

SECTION #8

1) Do you not take criticism well?
   ☐ YES   ☐ NO

2) Do you feel negative emotions when others tell you what to do?
   ☐ YES   ☐ NO

3) Do you dislike accepting change?
   ☐ YES   ☐ NO

4) Do you like to always get your way?
   ☐ YES   ☐ NO

If you answered "yes" to one or more of the questions in this section, you may be dealing with the issue of a lack of humility.

SECTION #9

1) Do you passionately dislike others around you?
   ☐ YES   ☐ NO

2) Do you wish to harm the people who have done you wrong?
   ☐ YES   ☐ NO

3) Do you dislike certain ethnic groups or certain types of people?
   ☐ YES   ☐ NO

4) Would you intentionally harm someone if there were no consequences behind it?
☐ YES   ☐ NO

5) Do you think you are better than some people?
☐ YES   ☐ NO

6) Would you consider yourself to be more fortunate than others?
☐ YES   ☐ NO

7) Do you judge others around you?
☐ YES   ☐ NO

8) Do you dislike dealing with people who you believe are not on your level?
☐ YES   ☐ NO

If you answered "yes" to one or more of the questions in this section, you may be dealing with issues of pride and arrogance.

SECTION #10

1) Do you tell lies when it is convenient?
☐ YES   ☐ NO

2) Do you make promises that you often break?
☐ YES   ☐ NO

3) Do you use words loosely to appease others around you?
   ☐ YES   ☐ NO

4) Do you at times pretend to be someone other than who you are?
   ☐ YES   ☐ NO

If you answered "yes" to one or more of the questions in this section, you may be dealing with issues of deceit and untrustworthiness.

SECTION #11

1) Do you dislike sharing what you have with others?
   ☐ YES   ☐ NO

2) Do you keep to yourself knowledge that can benefit others?
   ☐ YES   ☐ NO

3) Are you selfish with your possessions?
   ☐ YES   ☐ NO

4) Are you afraid to teach others what you know because they may surpass you?
   ☐ YES   ☐ NO

If you answered "yes" to one or more of those questions in this section, you may be dealing with issues or jealousy and insecurity.

SECTION #12

1) Do you act before considering the effects your actions may have on others?
   ☐ YES   ☐ NO

2) Is your life all about you and what you can get?
   ☐ YES   ☐ NO

3) Will you jeopardize others so you can advance?
   ☐ YES   ☐ NO

4) Do you care about what others do, say, or feel?
   ☐ YES   ☐ NO

If you answered "yes" to one or more questions in this section, you may be dealing with issues of self-centeredness and selfish ambition.

SECTION #13

1) When people say things that you don't like, are you unable to stay quiet?
   ☐ YES   ☐ NO

2) When you feel negative emotions such as anger or resentment, do you automatically react?
   ☐ YES   ☐ NO

3) Are you quick to use your fists to handle problems?
   ☐ YES   ☐ NO

4) Do you wear your feelings on your sleeve, so that it is easy to tell how you feel?
   ☐ YES   ☐ NO

If you answered "yes" to any of the questions in this section, you may be dealing with issues of rage and anger.

Now that you have answered the questions, go back, and review all the yes boxes you checked and check off the areas in the chart below that you may need to work on according to your answers.

SELF-REFLECTION AUDIT GRID

___Shame and Guilt - Section 1
___Self-Pity and Low Self-Esteem - Section 2
___Anger, Resentment, and Unforgiveness - Section 3
___Depression and Frustration - Section 4
___Codependency and Insecurity - Section 5
___Anxiety, Fear, Worry and Doubt – Section 6
___Jealousy – Section 7
___Lack of Humility – Section 8
___Pride and Arrogance – Section 9
___Deceit and Untrustworthiness – Section 10
___Jealousy and Insecurity – Section 11
___Self-Centeredness and Selfish-Ambition – Section 12
___Rage and Anger – Section 13

SELF-REFLECTION OF GOOD CHARACTER AUDIT

SECTION #1

1) Do you give to others or help them with no expectations in return?
   ☐ YES   ☐ NO

2) Do you treat others just as well as you treat yourself?
   ☐ YES   ☐ NO

3) Do you naturally have an interest in the well-being of others?
   ☐ YES   ☐ NO

SECTION #2

1) Do you make it a principle to always tell the truth?
   ☐ YES   ☐ NO

2) Do you avoid situations where you may have to compromise your integrity to appease others?
   ☐ YES   ☐ NO

3) Do you value the words you tell others and stand by them?
   ☐ YES   ☐ NO

SECTION #3

1) Are you faithful to others when you make commitments?
   ☐ YES   ☐ NO

2) Do you protect your friends from slander or destruction at all costs?
   ☐ YES   ☐ NO

3) Are you there for whom you love during both good times and bad times?
   ☐ YES   ☐ NO

SECTION #4

1) Are you modest when you are around others, treating people equally even if your achievements in life are more substantial than theirs?
   ☐ YES   ☐ NO

2) Do you acknowledge God as the Source of all good things in your life?
   ☐ YES   ☐ NO

3) Are you grateful for all that you have, even during difficult times?
   ☐ YES   ☐ NO

SECTION #5

1) Do you make it a principle to find ways to give back to others?
   ☐ YES   ☐ NO

2) When you see someone in need, do you extend a helping hand?
   ☐ YES   ☐ NO

3) Do you teach others the skill sets and talents you have learned?
   ☐ YES   ☐ NO

SECTION #6

1) Do you make it a policy to count your blessings on a regular basis?
   ☐ YES   ☐ NO

2) Are you generally pleasant and kind to others?
   ☐ YES   ☐ NO

3) Do you remain positive even when circumstances around you may seem negative?
   ☐ YES   ☐ NO

SECTION #7

1) Can you be counted on to perform the tasks and duties you have committed to?
   ☐ YES   ☐ NO

2) Do you take your promises seriously?
   ☐ YES   ☐ NO

3) Are you consistent in your performance and complete the task that you begin?
   ☐ YES   ☐ NO

SECTION #8

1) Do you wait patiently for your expected results?
   ☐ YES   ☐ NO

2) Is it easy for you to deal with others even when they are irrational?
   ☐ YES   ☐ NO

3) Are you able to pass up an urge if it is not the right time to fulfill it?
   ☐ YES   ☐ NO

SECTION #9

1) Do you treat others well even if they are not nice to you?
   ☐ YES   ☐ NO

2) Do you share positive words with others whom you interact?
   ☐ YES   ☐ NO

3) Do you do good things to people with no expectancy of return?
   ☐ YES   ☐ NO

SECTION #10

1) When others injure you, are you able to control your temper?
   ☐ YES   ☐ NO

2) Do you think about the consequences of your actions before you act?
   ☐ YES   ☐ NO

3) Do you try to rid yourself of negative thoughts when they creep in?
   ☐ YES   ☐ NO

SECTION #11

1) Do you make it a policy to keep positive thoughts in your mind even during adversity?
   ☐ YES   ☐ NO

2) Do you prefer a calm, tranquil environment?
   ☐ YES   ☐ NO

3) Do you encourage those around you to get along and to consider the needs of others?
   ☐ YES   ☐ NO

SECTION #12

1) Do you easily forgive others who have wronged you?
   ☐ YES   ☐ NO

2) Do you pray for your enemies and wish them the best?
   ☐ YES   ☐ NO

3) Are you compassionate toward others who have made mistakes and experienced hardships?
   ☐ YES   ☐ NO

   Now that you are finished answering the questions, go back and review all the boxes you checked "yes" to, and check off the areas in the chart below that describe your good attributes according to your answers.

SELF-REFLECTION CHARACTER STRENGTH GRID

___ Loving/Kind- Section 1
___Honest/Truthful - Section 2
___Loyal/Faithful - Section 3
___Humble/Content - Section 4
___Generous/ Helpful - Section 5
___Joyous/Positive – Section 6
___Trustworthy/Dependable – Section 7
___Patient/Calm – Section 8
___Kind/Compassionate – Section 9
___Self-controlled/Temperate – Section 10
___Peaceful/Peacemaker – Section 11
___Merciful/Forgiving – Section 12

CHAPTER FOUR
RELATIONSHIP PROCESS

Let's go back to a time when I was younger, five or six years old. I mentioned to you that on the right side of my house was a field where farmers planted crops. What I was able to glean from that entire process was that for you to build meaningful and sustainable relationships, just like a farmer must do, you must cultivate the landscape. You must prepare the landscape. Quite often as you are preparing the land, you must plow it. That is not always easy. Most often when you are trying to initiate a relationship with someone, you must come out of your comfort zone. As you are coming out of your comfort zone, sometimes you may experience some pain as you go through the process. Depending on how you grew up or your perception, perspective, or what you may have heard regarding other individuals, you might find the required plowing part of the process challenging. This plowing is a necessary means for growth. As you go about the process of plowing, you must make sure you fertilize as well, which means you must nurture the relationship from the very beginning. In essence, you end up having to use as your fertilizer, things such as grace and mercy and patience and understanding. Once you can do those things, now you are truly prepared to plant that seed, the relationship seed. Once you can plant that relationship seed, that is where the navigation and the cultivation of the relationship continues. It continues because you must make certain that the weeds do not come in and disrupt the germination process. You must make certain that you have an irrigation system and that you are watering the seed. Sometimes relationships become dry due to the lack of hydration such as patience, kindness, and respect. Sometimes the seed of relationships is naturally watered by treating others as we would like to be treated. However, there are times when you must bring in the irrigation system itself. You alone are responsible for determining precisely what you can do to enhance the probability of improving the relationship. These are things that we don't do as well because for various reasons we fail to self-reflect. This self-reflection is the key to unlocking our self-awareness which allows us to grow. In essence it allows us to remove the weeds that strangle meaningful relationships. As the relationship seed begins to germinate, we understand that during the growth process it is often necessary to come in and spray for weeds with pesticides. There is always going to be something that can disrupt or damage relationships in which one is invested. Especially meaningful relationships because we know vulnerability is important but sometimes scary. Relationships require vulnerability because we must be able to trust one another.

Another thing you're going to find in relationships is a certain aspect of pain. There is no relationship that you have and deem to be meaningful where there has not been a certain element of pain that has been experienced by those individuals engaged in the relationship. Relationship building is a process, just like farming. There are certain steps that you must take. Each and every step is extremely important, and I was able to learn that as I watched the farmers cultivate their crops. I was able to learn that as I watched the process of the seeds germinate and grow and become that soybean, wheat or corn.

Now, let's get back to the left side of my house regarding the school, which as I noted earlier was segregated at the time, I was able to observe the application of certain tenets and certain actionable tools required for relationships to flourish. I watched coaches go about the business of navigating and cultivating relationships and in the process, building trust. I watched coaches become vulnerable with the student-athletes while establishing relationships. I watched student-athletes be vulnerable and become vulnerable in their relationships with the coaches. I observed times where there was pain taking place as those relationships continued to be built upon. Most importantly, I watched the tools that were needed and required for those relationships to become meaningful and sustainable. We often talk to coaches about the idea of either being a coach for the moment or a coach for life. I have watched coaches go about being coaches for life as opposed to coaching for the moment. Once you initiate the process of relationship building, how do you then employ those actionable tools that are required to make sure your relationships are meaningful and sustainable. Some of the information provided is information gleaned over the years through some life changing experiences. These experiences through self-reflection have opened my eyes to the idea of becoming the best human being possible. That is the idea behind the story.

SELF-REFLECTION QUESTIONS:

1) Sometimes our biggest regrets are the people we have called friends. Do you have such a regret? If yes explain.

_____
_____
_____
_____
_____
_____
_____
_____
_____

2) How could you have salvaged the relationship?

_____
_____
_____
_____
_____
_____
_____
_____
_____

3) Name 5 things that are important to you regarding relationships you have with others.

_____
_____
_____
_____
_____
_____
_____
_____
_____

4) Do you provide the 5 qualities you listed to others in which you have a relationship? If yes how. If no what changes can you make.

_____
_____
_____
_____
_____
_____
_____
_____
_____
_____

CHAPTER FIVE
PURPOSE

I shared my upbringing; where I was born and who raised me. I also provided to you information about where I grew up and the neighborhood and the demographics of the neighborhood. I shared with you how my house was located within that neighborhood. What I did not share was the fact that out of all the homes in the neighborhood, although my house had a lot of love in it, we lacked a lot of amenities. My home was the only one in the neighborhood that did not have indoor plumbing. It did not have indoor bathrooms, or baths, or showers. We pumped water from an outdoor pump then would heat the water on a stove. This is how we warmed water for baths and to wash dishes and clean clothes. As a kid, ages five, six or seven, and dealing with fear demons especially at night, when I had need of a bathroom, I normally had to walk out twenty to twenty-five yards from the house just to use the outhouse (bathroom), regardless of the time at night or early morning. Kids can be mean and insensitive and there were times when I had to hear the jokes or was the brunt of some teasing. But that was the way that it was and that was what I was dealing with. Even with all that, the kids in the neighborhood would always migrate to my house. That is where we played. There were times when I was a little older and friends would come over, but they would not come inside the house. I grew up dealing with that from an early age. Perhaps it did not bother me as much because I was aware of how much love we had in the house. Maybe it did not bother me because when you do not have certain things you can't necessarily miss them. I did not take my first shower prior to the age of nine. So because of my lack of knowledge and lack of awareness regarding certain amenities, it never really bothered me. What is interesting is that I am more than certain there were individuals who rode past the house and individuals who lived in the neighborhood that perceived the kids growing up in that house in a particular fashion. One could conclude that their perception of us was one that we were not necessarily going to amount to much, maybe we could become farmhands and something of that sort. But that was my house not my home. You see the house lacked amenities, but my home had everything I would need, support, faith, hope and love. That was how I grew up. To this day, I do not regret any of that knowing what I know now.

One of the things that we always talk about is perception; how individuals perceive you and, what's more important, how you perceive yourself. Growing up with a lack of amenities, we never thought any less of one another and we never thought any less of ourselves. As a matter of fact, many individuals would say to you that I always walked with a certain air about myself. I always carried and conducted myself in a fashion where I didn't think anyone was better than myself regardless of race, creed, ethnicity, or socioeconomic status. Because of the way I perceived myself, I insisted that those who grew up in my house perceive themselves in the exact same way. So, why do I share this with you? I share this with you because at the end of the day when you are talking about purpose, one of the things that I know is that what precedes you finding your purpose or your purpose finding you is perception. The way other individuals see you and the way you see yourself.

Significance also precedes you finding your purpose or your purpose finding you. We will have an opportunity to discuss this later.

We often hesitate to seek that which is uncomfortable and justify it by settling on the idea that one's calling or purpose has to be found. However, various experiences lead me to wonder if we should seek our calling or will our purpose in life be revealed to us. Either way, whatever your purpose happens to be, you have been prepared for it.

So, I share this story with you because as you know by now, I was born and raised in Kinston, NC, which I always refer to as God's Country. Kinston, NC, has anywhere from 20,000 to 23,000 people. In the state of North Carolina, there are 10.5 to 11 million people that reside in the state. One of the things that most law enforcement officials are most proud of in the state is when they receive their Advanced Certificate. The Advanced Certificate is not based solely on their tenure. It is based on the amount of time they have served their community, the type of service they have provided their community, and the particular training they have received.

I remember when I received my Advanced Certificate. It was an extremely proud moment for me. It was an extremely proud moment because I saw my name on the certificate and I knew that it represented not only myself but also my family. Just as I did, most individuals who receive their Advanced Certificates feel a certain sense of pride, for various reasons. As I recall looking at my name and seeing my name on the certificate, I also recall the names of those individuals who were authorized to sign the certificates. The names of those individuals who could put their name on certificates that would be framed and hung on walls around all 100 counties within the state of North Carolina. I always thought that was very cool. I'd look at my name and the names of some of those individuals. During that time, there were only 31 individuals who were authorized to sign these certificates. So yes, I looked at my name with a lot of pride. What is interesting now is that out of 11 million people in the state of North Carolina, when others go about the business of looking at their certificates and see their names on it now, many individuals can actually find my name as well. You see out of 11 million people in the state of North Carolina, I became one of those 31 individuals authorized to sign it. Remember that boy who didn't even know the pleasure and convenience of a shower prior to the age of nine, the kid who had to go outside twenty to twenty-five yards in the middle of the night just to use the bathroom, who had no running water inside the house, who happened to be teased on occasion, whose friends were embarrassed to come into the house as we got older? Yes, that kid! So, does the perception of others and how individuals perceive you matter? Yes, one's perception of you does play a role to a certain extent. However, the most important thing is the perception you have of yourself. Eleven million individuals and I became one of the thirty-one. That has less to do with me and more about those individuals who believed in me. The individuals inside that house who believed in me, who always told me that I could do or be anything that I wanted to do or be and those individuals outside of that house who inspired me to seek opportunities and those who afforded me opportunities.

SELF-REFLECTION STORY:

Provide, in the space provided below a life story/experience that has influenced your perception of yourself, and what you perceive to be your purpose in life.

_____
_____
_____
_____
_____
_____
_____
_____
_____
_____
_____
_____
_____
_____
_____
_____
_____
_____
_____
_____

CHAPTER SIX
SIGNIFICANCE

On the other side of that field located on the right side of my childhood home, which was also part of the neighborhood, were neighbors who all happened to be white. As a matter of fact, my very first best friend was a white kid by the name of Dale Smith. I remember the first time that I saw Dale. There was nothing planted in the field and I was playing in the yard. I could see Dale on the other side of the field playing on these huge mounds of dirt. We used to refer to these mounds as the mountains. Early one morning, probably around 8:15 or 8:30, we made eye contact even though there was some distance between us. By midday, Dale and I found ourselves in the middle of the field playing. From that time moving forward, all the way through elementary school, every morning when we were not in school, I would always step out to see if Dale was on the mountains. Likewise, Dale would look to see if I was in the yard. As soon as we were both present, we would always go to the middle of the field and play. Eventually, I ended up at his house and quite often he ended up at my house. I am not going to suggest to you that we did not see color. That would not only be disingenuous but untrue. We saw color but it just did not matter, at least to us. We were just two five-year old kids who enjoyed doing some of the exact same things: playing in the dirt, playing with one another, wrestling, getting upset with one another or getting into fights where his mom or my grandmother would make us go apologize. Then we were right back at it the next day. In essence, we were doing what kids do.

On the left side of the house, on the other side of the school, that portion of the neighborhood was all black. Some of them were even relatives. So, I had my choice each day. I could always go to the right side and play with Dale and some other friends over there or I could go to the left side on the other side of the school and play with some relatives and friends over there. What was interesting is how the two sides never came together and played as neighborhood kids. They weren't familiar with one another. They had some idea of what they were, whether they lived on the left side or the right side, but they really didn't have any idea with regards to who they were. After some time passed, I was able to get both groups of the neighborhood to play together. There were times we would play in the field, especially when there were no crops. There were other times when we would go over to the school and play. Quite often, they would all meet at my grandparent's house and we would play in the yard. We would play football or basketball. Anytime we needed more space, we would play in the field or go over to the school. That is where I learned how to go about the business of building meaningful and sustainable relationships. I also learned from that experience that it is always important to learn *who* someone happens to be as opposed to *what* someone happens to be.

I learned that although I had a choice regarding who I played with and where I played, we do ourselves a disservice and fail to reach our full potential while also stunting our own growth when we isolate ourselves or others. I learned that by accepting being uncomfortable, which is often experienced when one attempts to connect others who resist establishing certain connections with those they deem different for various reasons, it is nevertheless an opportunity afforded to us to serve others. We introduce people to different food, clothing styles, art, music, books, etc… What better than to introduce and connect one human being with another? By doing so, the mind, heart and spirit is not only nourished but also expanded.

This is a service in which we are all capable of providing to one another. It was stated by Muhammad Ali in 1978 and accredited to others possessing greater understanding than I that, "Service is the rent we pay for existing on earth."

SELF-REFLECTION QUESTIONS:

1) Who has been the most significant person in your life and why?

   _____
   _____
   _____
   _____
   _____
   _____
   _____
   _____

2) How would your life be different if they had not been a presence in your life?

   _____
   _____
   _____
   _____
   _____
   _____
   _____
   _____

3) How do you think the lives of those for whom you have influenced in a positive manner would be different if you had not been there for them?

_____
_____
_____
_____
_____
_____
_____
_____
_____
_____

CHAPTER SEVEN
PURPOSEFUL EXPERIENCES, WHO ARE YOU?

When I was five years old, I received my first vehicle. Actually, I received two. One vehicle I received was a red Ford Fire Chief's vehicle. I played with that vehicle all the time. That vehicle would be over 50 years old right now. The other vehicle was a blue police cruiser. I spent a large part of my day playing with both of those cars. The red fire vehicle was a Ford while the blue police vehicle was a Chevrolet. My grandfather used to tell me, "Son, a Ford is built for longevity, but the Chevrolet is built for speed." Because of that, I became a huge Richard Petty fan. For those of you who do not know who Richard Petty is, he is still referred to today as the King of NASCAR. After he retired, I became a huge Dale Earnhardt fan because Dale also drove a Chevy. Interestingly enough, I still have the red Fire Chief vehicle. It is not mint condition, but I still have it, over 50 years later. Therefore, I guess my grandfather was correct about the longevity of a Ford. The police vehicle, I no longer have and there is a reason why. You see, I rolled the police vehicle down my grandparent's porch. I would take the vehicle and throw it against trees and up in the air. I guess one could say I mistreated that vehicle to a certain extent but that was okay. Because the individuals, in my mind and imagination, who happened to be in that vehicle were superheroes. So, no matter what I did to the vehicle, there was no way that the individuals who inhabited that vehicle would ever be injured. You see, firemen do a fantastic job and they save lives and yes are heroes. But for me as a kid, they still weren't the same type of heroes as those who were a part of law enforcement.

I often say that I responded to my first call at the age of six years old. While riding my bike out in the yard, my grandmother was on the back porch washing clothes. We heard this huge bang. Neither of us knew what it was. My grandmother asked me to ride my bike down the road to see what that noise was all about. This was during the time in our country when at the age of six, seven or eight, a young person could take their bike and ride it and be gone most of the morning, yet the parents knew their child was okay. I went darting out of the yard onto the road and I was riding as fast as I could so I could come back and report to my grandmother exactly what that noise happened to be. As I was approaching not quite a half mile down the road, I saw a tractor trailer truck and then I could also see a vehicle. I proceeded to continue down the road and upon my arrival it appeared that the tractor trailer truck attempted to merge back on to the highway. Maybe the driver had pulled over late the previous night to go to sleep. We found out later that the young lady who happened to be in the vehicle was on her way to a Dupont plant which was just outside of Kinston. As I got closer, I could see everything that had taken place. I remember looking at the vehicle and seeing the lady inside the vehicle. She was virtually decapitated. She was mangled inside the vehicle. I remember looking at the road and I could see some oil and transmission fluid and gas. I could also see other fluids too. Like a darkish red and I could only surmise that this fluid came from her. I was the first to respond to that call and I was six years old. No six-year-old should have to see sights such as that. To my knowledge I never had nightmares. I never really told individuals what I saw. I never even told them how I felt when I saw it or how I felt afterwards. To be honest, it has been so long ago that I don't know if I could begin to tell you exactly how I felt neither. But for me, that was the first call that I ever responded to.

At the age of nine, I was awakened early one morning, about 2 a.m., because there was a thud in the kitchen. As I got up, I heard screaming. I walked down the hall into the kitchen, and I saw my grandfather lying on the floor. One of my uncles was providing CPR to him. That was the first time I ever learned anything regarding CPR. Then, I remember hearing the sirens drawing near. When they arrived and placed my grandfather on the gurney, they appeared to be working on him. Once he was placed into the ambulance, it dawned on me that the ambulance didn't leave.

They were speaking with the state trooper and state inspector who lived on the right side of my house on the other side of the field. I knew their kids as well and often played with their kids. I remember one of them trying to console my grandmother. I also remember thinking to myself, why aren't they taking my grandfather to the hospital so he can get the help he needs. A few minutes later, the ambulance pulled out of the yard and had on the sirens. I could hear them because the sirens were so loud. But then I noticed that the sirens were turned off. And I never understood that.

As I got older, I realized that there was no reason for them to continue with the sirens because my grandfather had died on the kitchen floor. How all these things affected me...I have absolutely no idea. I can tell you to this very day that any time I see an ambulance, it is not the most pleasing thing to me because I think about where they are going and who they are transporting. I know that if I have any type of fear whatsoever it is being placed in an ambulance. Who knows, at some point and time maybe I will be. These were some experiences I had at an early age. For some, perhaps the events could be classified as trauma but for me through self-reflection these experiences are viewed as uncomfortable moments that shaped me into the individual I am today. Sure, I saw and witnessed things at a young age that I would not want others at such a young age to experience, however, I learned not to focus upon the event but to focus upon how my experiences could possibly help others. I do not wish any of these experiences on anyone.

We often say that it is not necessarily the case that we find our purpose. Sometimes our purpose finds us. Whatever that purpose happens to be and however the two connect, you and your purpose, if you reflect, what you will realize is that you've been prepared for whatever your purpose happens to be. For me, it was always about serving others and putting others before myself. That is my makeup and that is who I am. The perception that I've always had of me has been simple. Due to the significant role that my grandfather played in my life and that all my loved ones have played in my life, I understand that I am also significant in the life of someone. That preparation, which I've shared with you, and my purpose…is exactly what I am doing with my life. Prayerfully, you will find this information helpful regarding establishing meaningful relationships. The goal is to assist individuals to understand earnestly the importance of communication, the significance of self-reflection when trying to determine what their calling may be, and first and foremost their purpose in life. Mark Twain once said, "The two most important or significant times in one's life, is the day that you are born and the day you realize why."

SELF-REFLECTION EXPERIENTIAL

Helping
Other
People
Excel

Make a list of 5 people who have helped you up to this point and provided you with hope.

Provide in your list specifics regarding how they helped you, then commit to helping others by providing them with the same actionable assistance in which you were provided.

_____
_____
_____
_____
_____
_____
_____
_____
_____
_____
_____
_____
_____
_____
_____
_____
_____

Self-reflection is the key to self-awareness which is ultimately required to attain social awareness. Social awareness is essential in our efforts to learn to understand where others are in their life excursion. We often insist that people meet us where we are rather than taking the time to meet individuals where they are in life. When we take the time, which we refer to as giving others their twenty seconds, it reminds us to take the time to listen to others. Listening allows us to better understand and acknowledge the experiences and individual perceptions which drive and influence the beliefs of others.

Taking the time to prepare one's self to empathize and place one's self in the shoes of others is a great human characteristic but understanding that doing so does not allow us to experience every step that individual has taken is wisdom in which only human beings have been blessed.

Therefore, you owe it to yourself to truly understand who you are and to provide others their twenty seconds for you to get to know who they are internally rather than assuming what they are based upon the external. In the end, this is about us being human beings and made in God's image. We must find within ourselves the ability to tap into the humanness which we all possess and express it to one another with grace, mercy, kindness, understanding and love. Imagine if we could all commit to the idea of HOPE.

Galatians 3:28

There is neither Jew nor Gentile, neither slave nor free, nor is there male and female, for you are all one in Christ Jesus.

This speaks to me as a devout Christian. But, whatever your faith, the message is clear: we must look beyond differences. When we proclaim "them versus us" or "they versus them", we tap into our worst nature. We are not perfect beings, but we are better human beings than we have often shown. There is no way that one can become a better human being and not serve one another better, regardless of our capacity, role, or title.

ACKNOWLEDGEMENT

The making of this book has been a collaboration of relationships from childhood to present. These relationships and interactions inspired aspirations which could not have been imagined without the love, nurturing and support of so many. I could separate them into categories such as family, friends, coaches, educators, mentors, role models and many others, however, they all fall into one specific category. They are human beings designed to be in my life by God, responsible for who I am rather than what I am.

There are times when we may conclude that our biggest regret is certain individuals we have allowed in our lives. It is in our interest to self-reflect and think of the lessons that we learned from our biggest regrets as well. By doing so, it makes it easier to love them and even forgive them if necessary. Therefore, I would like to acknowledge everyone with whom I have had interaction but most importantly, I acknowledge God for loving me enough to place them all in my sphere and using them to mold me into who I am. I am imperfect but striving to honor all who have honored me with their time, effort, laughter, tears, and prayers. I have been able to learn from my failures by seeing each failure as a pathway to success, learn from my pain how to connect with humanity and learn from my fears how to summon the strength we all possess. What a joy it is to be a part of humanity when our lives are rooted in faith, hope, love, and a real commitment to honor one another and to be bound by togetherness.

DEDICATION

This book is dedicated to Carolyn, Jaymee, Matthew, Jacob, John, Nicole, and Jaelyn. As my wife and kids, my goal has been to love, serve and protect you. I hope that you have seen my spiritual growth over the years and my desire to love you all unconditionally. Thank you for keeping me alert and grounded. Thank you for making me so proud of who you are and your commitment to one another. Thank you for allowing me to learn from you and at least pretending to be interested in my back in the day stories. I love you all so much.

REFERENCES:

Muhammad Ali, Times Magazine, (1978)
Carl Jung, Memories, Dreams, Reflections, (1989)
Mark Twain, Quotes on Life, Politics, Travel and More by Amy Finn, (2022)
Jamila T. Davis, Voices of Consequences Workbook Journal, (2012)
New International Version NIV Bible Gateway

Made in the USA
Columbia, SC
30 June 2025